With all,

Mindy

To: _____

From: _____

Date: _____

Message: _____

_____

_____

_____

# To Mom, with Love

Jack Canfield, Mark Victor Hansen

**Health Communications, Inc.**
**Deerfield Beach, Florida**

*www.hcibooks.com*
*www.chickensoup.com*

**Library of Congress Cataloging-in-Publication Data
is available from the Library of Congress**

©2006 Jack Canfield, Mark Victor Hansen
ISBN 0-7573-0478-8

Publisher:  Health Communications, Inc.
            3201 S.W. 15th Street
            Deerfield Beach, FL 33442–8190

*Cover and inside book design by Larissa Hise Henoch*
*Photos ©Shutterstock*

# May Morning

I lie stretched out upon the window-seat
And doze, and read a page or two, and doze,
And feel the air like water on me close,
Great waves of sunny air that lip and beat
With a small noise, monotonous and sweet,
Against the window—and the scent of cool,
Frail flowers by some brown and dew-drenched pool
Possesses me from drowsy head to feet.

This is the time of all-sufficing laughter
At idiotic things some one has done,
And there is neither past nor vague hereafter.
And all your body stretches in the sun
And drinks the light in like a liquid thing;
Filled with the divine languor of late spring.

—Stephen Vincent Benét

# Motherhood:
## A Transformation

Once upon a time I was a nurse, a writer and a wife. Then one day, I had a child. I became a mother.

Added to the list of things I previously was, I became a chauffeur, a cook, a dresser, a wiper of dirty faces, a cleaner of soiled diapers, a retriever of thrown socks, a finder of lost shoes, a doer of homework, an insomniac. I was a referee in toy wars, a slayer of nighttime dragons, a soother of nervous school jitters. I was a room mother, a den mother, a leader of Girl Scouts and one day, mother of the bride. I calmed tantrums and bolstered fragile egos.

With each passing day my talents grew: I became a baker of cookies, a sewer of Halloween costumes extraordinaire. I could braid hair in the time most people wash their faces. And I could smile even when I didn't want to.

Where once my body had been my own to do with as I pleased, it now belonged to someone else. It became a breast to nourish at, a shoulder to cry on, a lap to sit and cuddle upon. My lips became the kissers of boo-boos, my hips the transporters of small, squirmy bundles. My feet were now used to walk the floor at all hours of the night, my arms became a cradle. I grew eyes in the back of my head, and my hearing became supersonic.

Once upon a time my name was Peggy. Then I became a mother and had as many aliases as a con man. I became—at various times—Mm, Ma-ma, Ma,

Mommie, Mom, Mother, MOTHER! And for a brief period of mental vexation, "Peg."

My mind, which used to flourish with egocentric thoughts, now became filled with irrational ideations: *What if she falls out of the crib? What if he chokes on his food? What if I do or say the wrong thing? How will I know I'm a good parent? How will I know I'm a bad one?*

My house, once so orderly and tidy, became a disorderly jumble of toys and stuffed animals, dried peas and empty, strewn formula bottles; a carpet of clutter and chaos; a dwelling of disarray.

My heart, once only given to another, was now taken from me and filled to the brim, bursting with devotion and love.

I was a Mother. I was an icon. I'd done something no man had ever done, accomplished a feat so death defying and magical that many wouldn't even attempt it. I became a Mother. And in so doing, I became all that I was, all that I ever wished to be.

*Peggy Jaeger*
*(Chicken Soup for Every Mom's Soul)*

Mom, I love you because you make me laugh.

# The Origins of Mother's Day

The earliest version of Mother's Day was in ancient Greece where, in the springtime, people celebrated the goddess, Rhea, who was the mother of all gods. At dawn they would offer her honey cakes, fine drinks and flowers.

## Greek Honey Cake

INGREDIENTS:

1 cup all-purpose flour
1½ teaspoons baking
   powder
¼ teaspoon salt
½ teaspoon cinnamon
2 teaspoon orange zest
¾ cup butter
¾ cup white sugar

3 eggs
¼ cup milk
1 cup chopped walnuts

1 cup white sugar
1 cup honey
¾ cup water
1 teaspoon lemon juice

DIRECTIONS:

Preheat oven to 350°. Grease and flour a 9-inch cake pan.

In a bowl, combine the flour, baking powder, salt, cinnamon and orange rind. Set aside.

In another large bowl, cream together the butter and ¾ cup sugar until light and fluffy.

One at a time, beat in the eggs and add the orange zest.

Mix in the dry ingredients, alternating with the milk, just until incorporated.

Stir in the walnuts.

Pour batter into prepared pan and bake for 40 minutes, or until a toothpick inserted into the center of the cake comes out clean. Allow to cool for 15 minutes and cut the cake into diamond shapes.

HONEY SYRUP:

In a saucepan, combine honey, 1 cup of sugar and water. Bring to a simmer and cook for 5 minutes, constantly stirring. Stir in lemon juice, bring to a boil and cook for 2 minutes.

Pour honey syrup over the cake.

# The Baby Book

When I was a little girl, I loved looking through my baby book. I would sit nestled on my mother's lap, while she carefully turned the pages for me. She read my name out loud. She read her name, my father's name, my grandparents' names. She read the date and time of my birth. She let me look inside the little envelope with a lock of my baby hair in it. My favorite part of the book was at the very end. It was three pages of photographs, and I was in every single one. The photos were slipping behind the clear plastic that refused to hold them in place and the plastic on one page was torn. This did not bother me in the least. I loved to look at the pictures of my mother holding the newborn me. When one photo slid behind another, my mother would pull it out, and I laughed in excitement as the hidden treasure was revealed.

Now I am a mother with a daughter of my own. As I put together a baby book for my daughter, I keep looking back into my own book. However, my baby book no longer looks the same. When I look at the photo of my mother bathing me, I notice that she looks tired—as I feel now. When I look carefully into the background of the photos, I see that my mother's kitchen had cluttered counters— like my kitchen has now. I see photos of my smiling, happy face in a bathtub, oblivious to the clutter and my mother's fatigue—just as my baby smiles now.

And I notice one other change in the book. There was always a section of pages in the middle of the book that were never written in. These are the blank pages that I hear my new mother friends complain about. I hear mothers guiltily complain that they have not filled in all of the pages of the baby book yet. I hear mothers criticizing themselves, saying that it will be depressing if their child sees blank pages in her baby book. But as I look back in my baby book, I see that all of the blank pages have suddenly disappeared. Where the blank pages once lay, I now see my mother cooking me warm, nourishing meals and giving me hot baths. I see my mother reading me books and taking me sledding in the front yard. I see my mother tucking me into bed and bandaging my skinned knee. I see pages full of love.

*Julie Bete*
(Chicken Soup for the Mother and Daughter Soul)

*A mother's hugs
are the best hugs
there are.*

*Mother's intuition can tell you everything with kids. Mothers have a sixth sense. You're in tune with your child. You can hear them calling for help.*

—Jane Seymour

# Lessons on Napkins

My mother was an excellent student and wanted to be a special education teacher. But her dreams of becoming a teacher were interrupted by an unexpected child: her own. My mother became pregnant with me during her junior year of college and left school to marry my father. Yet even though my mother left the field of education formally, she did not leave it entirely.

When I finally entered a school classroom at age five, I was excited but terrified. That first day of kindergarten, I quietly sat at my desk during snack time and opened my Miss Piggy lunch box. Inside the lunch box I found a note from my mother written on a napkin. The note said that she loved me, that she was proud of me and that I was the best kindergartner in the world! Because of that napkin note I made it through my first day of kindergarten . . . and many more school days to follow.

There have been many napkin notes since the first one. There were napkin notes in elementary school when I was struggling with math, telling me to "Hang in there, kiddo! You can do it! Don't forget what a great writer you are!" There were napkin notes in junior high school when I was the "new girl" with frizzy hair and pimples, telling me to "Be friendly. Don't be scared. Anyone would be lucky to have you as her friend!" In high school, when my basketball team was the first team in our school's history to play in a state championship, there were napkin notes telling me, "There is no 'I' in team. You have gotten this far because you know how to share." And there were even napkin notes sent to me in college and graduate school, far away from my mother's physical touch. Despite the tumultuous changes of college—changing majors, changing boyfriends, changing the way I looked at the world—my one constant was my mother's encouragement, support and teachings, echoed in years of love, commitment and napkin notes.

For Christmas this year, my mother received a book bag, a daily planner, notebooks and a full-tuition college scholarship. These gifts reflected an impending change in her life. After a twenty-five-year hiatus, my forty-four-year-old mother was finally going back to school to earn her degree in teaching. And although I was immensely proud of my mother for following her dreams, I wanted her to know that she didn't need a degree to make her a stellar teacher.

So I also gave her a Christmas gift for school: a lunch bag filled with her favorite foods. She laughed as she opened the lunch bag and took out cans of tuna fish and V-8. Then she pulled out a napkin with writing on it.

As she opened up her "You can do it!" napkin note from me, tears began running down her face. When her eyes met mine, I saw she understood my unspoken message: My mother is— and has always been—a teacher.

*Caurie Anne Miner*
(Chicken Soup for the Mother's Soul 2)

## *Ways to Make Your Kids' School Lunches Fun*

- Use large cookie cutters to cut their sandwich into a fun shape!

- Instead of regular bread, use a soft tortilla shell, pita bread, a bagel or leftover pancakes!

- Slice cheese, lunchmeat or pepperoni into little squares and place between crackers. You can also put peanut butter and jelly or peanut butter and banana slices on crackers!

- Cut cooked hot dogs into little pieces and send with ketchup packs for dipping.

- Pack tortilla chips and a small container of salsa for nachos on the go!

- Leftover pizza . . . kids love it cold!

- Pack carrot and celery sticks with a small container of ranch dressing for dipping.

- Make kabobs out of pieces of fruit, vegetables and cheese.

*The mother's
heart is the child's
schoolroom.*

# Mother's Lessons Can Last a Lifetime

I have learned many things from my mother. I learned where to go for comfort and sustenance as first I suckled at her breast, later climbed into her lap and now sit across the table from her with a cup of coffee.

I learned not to run into the road, not to touch the stove, not to run with scissors in my hand, never to use a BB gun lest I put my eye out, and that young ladies don't make impolite noises in public.

I learned that "please" and "thank you" are the most important words in the language, to respect my elders, to look a person in the eye when I speak, to sit with my knees together and keep my skirt down, and that a body must be bathed on Saturday night whether it needs it or not.

I learned to fry chicken, bake a cake, make sun tea, flip pancakes, can vegetables and wash dishes—by hand. I learned that "casserole" and "crock pot" are the most important words in kitchen language if you have hopes of pursuing any interests in life away from the stove.

Growing up on a farm, I also learned how to reach under the hens to gather eggs, how to avoid the rooster and the goose, how to pull ticks out of dogs, where to find a nest of baby bunnies in the spring, how to call to the bobwhite down by the creek, and to stay away from sows and their litters.

From my mother I also learned to look for the subtle

colors of the flowers in her garden, to listen to the mocking-bird's song in the morning, to enjoy the fragrance of the lilac, to spot the rainbow-rimmed moon and to play with the ladybug.

I learned, at her suggestion, that when I wasn't able to tell her the things that troubled me, I could write them to her, pouring out my heart on the sheets of a Big Chief writing tablet.

I learned that even though I sometimes hated her in adolescent rage, she always loved me. I learned that she didn't always have the right answer, but she always had the right intention. I learned that even though the crop didn't do well or the hay barn burned down or the cows got into the neighbor's corn field, you take care of things and go on.

My mother is sixty-seven now. She recently was diagnosed with cancer, underwent surgery and is receiving chemotherapy treatments.

And this is what I'm still learning from her: You can't always choose what experiences you'll face in life, but you can choose how you'll face them. That faith is stronger than fear, that the love of family and friends is powerful, that each day is a gift and that the fortunate daughter never stops learning from her mother.

*Vicki Marsh Kabat*
(Chicken Soup for Every Mom's Soul)

*Mom, your sense of humor brings light into my life.*

*Of* all the rights of women,
the greatest is to be a mother.

—Lin Yutang

# The Rocker

I stumbled with exhaustion, searching for the ringing telephone. Colicky three-month-old Max slept only two hours at a time, and my husband was away traveling again. My fatigued body ached. I found the phone under a receiving blanket and answered it.

My mother asked, "Is Max sleeping any better?"

"A little."

"You're not getting any sleep, are you?" She sounded worried.

My gritty eyes burned. "Not much."

"That must be so hard."

My throat closed. "Oh Mom, I'm exhausted! I can hardly think."

"I'm coming up."

Outside my window a December blizzard moaned through the darkness. My mother would have to navigate icy canyon roads to reach my house. I said, "It's snowing hard here. Don't come. I'll be okay."

"I'm on my way." She hung up. Tears of exhaustion and relief blurred my vision. My mother has always been my rock.

The usual thirty-minute drive took her an hour. My mother arrived looking rosy-cheeked from the cold, snow frosting her reddish-brown hair. She took baby Max from my arms and ordered me to bed. I said, "But Max needs to eat in the night."

She shook her head. "I know how to warm up formula.

Go to bed!" Her determined look told me not to argue.

My soft pillow beckoned to me, along with my cozy down comforter. I headed upstairs feeling relieved, but lying in bed I couldn't sleep. Guilt overwhelmed me. I should be able to take care of my baby. At least I could have offered to help. My mother wouldn't have let me, I realized. I heard her coo to Max as she climbed the stairs. Soon the rocking chair in baby Max's room creaked, back and forth, back and forth.

Suddenly I remembered my mother rocking me when I had the chicken pox. I was too big for rocking, but blisters invaded my throat, my ears, even the back of my eyelids. As we rocked my mother sang, "Rock-a-bye my big-big girl." The monotonous chant comforted me. I slept. When I woke in the night my mother offered sips of water and laid cold washrags across my burning forehead. I slept fitfully, but in the morning the blisters had crusted, and I felt better.

Now I could hear my mother chanting to Max, "Rock-a-bye my ba-by boy." Her monotone relaxed me, just as it had when I was a child. I slid toward sleep, knowing my baby was in capable hands. In the morning, I'd hug my mother, thank her, and tell her how her love had rocked both Max and me to sleep.

*Kendeyl Johansen*
(Chicken Soup for the Mother and Daughter Soul)

*M*otherhood:
*All love begins and ends there.*

—Robert Browning

## Famous "Motherisms"

Don't cross your eyes or
they'll stick that way.

Just wait 'til your father gets home!

Anything worth doing is worth doing right.

When you have kids of your own, I hope
they turn out just like you!

Because I said so, that's why.

Keep crying and I'll give you something to cry about!

I brought you into this world and I can take you out!

Good things come to those who wait.

Call me when you get there, just so I know you're okay.

I will always love you—no matter what.

Eat your vegetables, they're good for you.

Don't stay up too late!

Don't use that tone with me!

*A* mother's wrath does not survive the night.

—Burundi Proverb

*Mom, I love you even though you nag me all the time.*

# Forever, for Always
## and No Matter What!

Our daughter Ariana moved from baby to toddler with her share of the usual bumps and scraped knees. On these occasions, I'd hold out my arms and say, "Come see me." She'd crawl into my lap, we'd cuddle, and I'd say, "Are you my girl?" Between tears she'd nod her head yes. Then I'd say, "My sweetie, beetie Ariana girl?" She'd nod her head, this time with a smile. And I'd end with, "And I love you forever, for always and no matter what!" With a giggle and a hug, she was off and ready for her next challenge.

Ariana is now four-and-a-half. We've continued "come see me" time for scraped knees and bruised feelings, for "good mornings" and "good nights."

A few weeks ago, I had "one of those days." I was tired, cranky and overextended taking care of a four-year-old, twin teenage boys and a home business. Each phone call or knock at the door brought another full day's worth of work that needed to be done immediately! I reached my breaking point in the afternoon and went into my room for a good cry. Ariana soon came to my side and said, "Come see me." She curled up beside me, put her sweet little hands on my damp cheeks and said, "Are you my mommy?" Between my tears I nodded my head yes. "My sweetie, beetie mommy?" I nodded my head and smiled. "And I love you forever, for always and no matter what!" A giggle, a big hug, and I was off and ready for my next challenge.

*Jeanette Lisefski*
(Chicken Soup for the Mother's Soul)

*Mom,*
*I love you more*
*than a million*
*colors!*

## Relaxing "Mom"ents

Take a nice long walk.

Watch a funny movie or TV show.

Take a hot bubble bath surrounded
with scented candles.

Soak your feet.

Listen to your favorite CD.

Arrange a pretty bouquet of flowers.

*G*od could not be
everywhere. Therefore
he made mothers.

—Jewish Proverb

# The Mirror Has
# Three Faces

I am fifty-one years old. My mother was fifty-one when she died. I remember that last day of her life only too clearly. It was a rainy Monday, and my mother could not breathe.

"It's fluid," the doctor said. "We'll tap her lungs." They sat my mother up in the hospital bed and plunged the long needle through her back into her lungs. Again and again they tried, but no fluid came. And no relief.

"It's not fluid," the doctor said. "It's all tumor. We can't help her breathe."

I remember my mother's desperate words. "I can't . . . breathe. Turn up the oxygen . . . please." But turning up the oxygen didn't help. Her lungs, bursting with cancer, fought to make room for the air. My mother whispered her final words to me, "I want the quickest way."

My mother should have grown old. Her dark hair, peppered with gray, should have become snowy white. The fine lines, etched in her face from her smiles, should have become soft wrinkles. Her quick step should have given way to a slower, more seasoned gait.

My mother should have watched her five grandchildren grow up. She should have had the chance to enfold them in her very special brand of love and to impart to them her considerable wisdom. She should have been arm in arm with my father—she was the only girl he ever loved—sojourning into their shared golden years. She didn't. She wasn't. She never had the chance. She was fifty-one, and she died.

I was twenty-seven when my mother died. Over the years, not a day went by when I didn't think of something I wanted to tell her, to ask her or to show her. I railed bitterly against the injustice of it. It wasn't fair that my mother died at fifty-one.

Now I am fifty-one. I look into the mirror, and it strikes me: I have slowly but surely been transformed. There she is with that gray peppered hair, those dark, intense eyes, that expression on my face. When I hear my voice, it is her voice. I have become my mother.

I am entering a new and strange stage of my life. I have always looked ahead to see my mother. Ever so briefly, I stood next to her. Now I'm beginning to be older than my mother. The direction in which I gaze to see her will change. Soon I will look back at my mother.

Gradually my mother will become young in comparison with me. I will grow old instead of her—acquire the white hair she should have had but never did. I will develop that seasoned gait she never experienced, see those soft facial wrinkles she never had, and so it will continue on and on until one day when I'm seventy-five, as she would have been today. On that day, the reversal of our roles complete, I will turn around to look at her, but see instead my own daughter, at fifty-one—my mother.

*Kristina Cliff-Evans*
(Chicken Soup for the Golden Soul)

*M*irror Mirror on the Wall
*I Am My Mother After All*

—Stitched on a Pillow

*Mom, you're the best mom in the whole wide world!*

# *Famous Mothers*

Mother Hubbard

Mother Goose

Mother Teresa

Abigail Adams

Rose Kennedy

Mother Nature

Mother Earth

Mary

Mother Jones

Marie Curie

Rosa Parks

Eleanor Roosevelt

Sarah

# *Mothering Sunday*

The English tradition of "Mothering Sunday" is centuries old. Celebrated on the fourth Sunday of Lent, it was a day when children who worked as domestic servants were given the day off to visit their mothers and families. As they walked the country lanes to return home, the children would pick wild flowers and violets as gifts for their mothers.

# Violets

There are more than 400 species of violets in the world. Violets are perennials, with heart-shaped leaves that flower in the spring. The leaves of violets are edible when cooked and are also rich in vitamins. The flowers can be used to decorate meals. Flowers, leaves and roots are also used for medical purposes.

## Recipe for a Violet-Scented Bubble Bath

INGREDIENTS:

1 quart (4 cups) distilled water
1 (4 oz.) bar castile soap *(grated)*
   *(1 cup of unscented shampoo can be substituted.)*
2 ounces coconut oil
2 ounce liquid glycerin *(skin moisturizer)*
4 drops violet fragrant oil or violet perfume

DIRECTIONS:

Mix all ingredients together. Store in a plastic container.
Pour into running warm water.
Sit back and relax.

*NOTE: Castile soap, liquid glycerin and coconut oil can be found at health food stores and some drug stores.*

# Calling Mr. Clean

Maybe it was nesting on steroids. Possibly it was my less-than-neat twin toddlers. Or perhaps it was a compulsive desire to maintain the illusion of order in my life. Whatever the reason, during my last pregnancy, I just could not stop thinking about cleaning things. I just couldn't get enough of All Things Immaculate.

So when I saw the sponge, yellow, five inches thick and really squishy looking, I had to have it. Had to have it in a way only a pregnant woman has to have something. It's bizarre, but I actually salivated when I saw it. Had I ever seen anything more useful, more amazing? And for a mere ninety-nine cents! Who could pass up such a bargain? Certainly not pregnant old Pavlovian me.

Myriad cleaning endeavors starring the sponge and myself tap-danced glitzily around in my head. I would try it out first as my own personal bath implement. Unfortunately, it made a squeaky noise as I pulled it across my skin, so I had to nix that idea. I used it to clean the bathtub instead. After that, I couldn't stop thinking about it. I'd giddily daydream, planning our next encounter. Maybe tonight it would be the bathtub again. Or the kitchen floor. Or maybe even the car.

And it didn't stop with the sponge. Other cleaning implements, things that I hadn't glanced at in years, let alone used, became tantalizingly attractive to me. The white scouring brush under the sink. Brillo pads. Bottled cleaning products. I couldn't keep my hands off them.

At the supermarket, instead of pondering ice-cream bars in the frozen foods aisle as usual, I stood transfixed by Ajax, Soft Scrub and Pine Sol. Mr. Clean winked seductively at me, and I fantasized about just how sparklingly clean I could get my bathroom faucet if only I brought the burly fellow home with me.

I scoured the finish off the linoleum in the kitchen one night. I washed the car every day for a week. Masked and gloved, I obsessively sprayed, spritzed, rubbed, wiped, waxed and polished my way through my last trimester.

And then I had my baby boy, and the romance was over. Whatever hormone it was that caused my sponge fetish thankfully exited my body with my son, leaving me once again a comfortable slob, unconcerned about suds and sparkling appliances. The scrub brush got tossed back under the sink with a shrug; the brigade of impulse-purchased cleaning supplies was relegated to the back of the linen closet. I stopped returning Mr. Clean's calls. The wonder-sponge sulkily disappeared into the basement.

And then a couple of days ago, we were at Sam's Club, and there it was. Another sponge. A big, meaty, make-everything-sparkling-clean yellow sponge. My heart skipped a beat. I could practically taste the bone-tingling satisfaction of a cleaning job done right. I started to drool.

And that's when I knew.

That sponge and I were going to be very busy for the next nine months.

*Karen C. Driscoll*
(Chicken Soup for Every Mom's Soul)

# The Nesting Instinct

Development of a "nesting instinct" is common among pregnant women. Certain moms-to-be suddenly get an uncontrollable urge to clean the house from top to bottom, replacing all their towels and sheets with brand-new ones, rearranging the cupboards or the contents of the refrigerator, removing the baseboards just to clean behind them, and folding and refolding the baby's clothes. For those family members who feel the urge to get out of the house lest they get dragged into this cleaning spree, they can take comfort in knowing that this phenomenon usually ends with the baby's birth.

## *Make Cleaning Fun*

Clean as a team

Make it a game

Listen to your favorite music

Take breaks in between tasks

Do your least favorite task first

# The Unwrapped Gift

"Mom," came the frantic call from my teenage daughter's bedroom, "Come here quick!"

I opened one eye, still tired from the last-minute details of Christmas Eve and was on my feet just as Jennifer cried out again. Waves of dizziness struck me, almost knocking me back into bed. *What was going on?*

I managed to make it to my daughter and saw her sitting up, pale-faced and holding her stomach. She looked like I felt.

"What's the matter, Jennifer?" I asked.

"Mom, I've got the stomach flu, and it's Christmas!"

"Well, if it's any consolation, I don't feel so great myself." And, with that, I ran to the bathroom. I lay on the cold tile and thought, *Oh, God, why today of all days? Not today, Lord, not today.*

By now, my husband, hearing all the commotion, was up preparing breakfast. He assumed our noisy hoopla was the excitement of Christmas morning. Popping his head into the bathroom he said, "Bacon and eggs are on when you're ready." A closer look and he discovered his faux pas and slipped quietly back out of the room.

Our other two children went to church with him while Jennifer and I moaned encouragement to each other across the hall. After an hour of this, I thought, *This is silly . . . we certainly can't catch anything from each other, so why not bunk together?*

Jennifer came and got in our king-size bed with me. We spent the day talking, sucking ice chips and sleeping. When we were awake, we talked about boys, life at her new high school and friends she had made when she had changed schools midyear.

I told her how hard it was to be a working mother and still stay on top of all the family activities. I confessed that I had missed sharing with her lately, and we made a pact to spend more time together. We told each other secrets, giggled and laughed at our predicament. We became closer that day than we had been in a long time.

Many years have passed, and my daughter is grown with a husband and two children of her own. Yet not a Christmas goes by that one of us doesn't say, "Remember the Christmas when . . . ?" We both laugh, knowing we received a gift that year better than any we found under the tree.

*Sallie Rodman*

(Chicken Soup for the Mother and Daughter Soul)

## *Gifts You Might Not Have Thought Of . . .*

- Make a donation to a favorite charity.

- Write a letter telling your friend how much she means to you. Solicit other friends and family members to do the same.

- Make a book of coupons for services you can provide, such as a home-cooked meal, a night of babysitting or to run an errand.

- Put together a photo album or scrapbook containing old pictures.

- Create a basket of goodies containing fresh baked cookies, homemade candies or different kinds of muffins.

- If you're artistic, paint or draw a picture representing something special. Have it nicely framed.

- Whisk your friend away to a spa or beauty salon to be pampered at your expense.

- Take your friend to a play, concert or movie that she's been dying to see.

- Give her a night off by keeping her children at your house for the night, then work with the children to create a special gift for their mother.

- Send a nice plant or dried flower arrangement that will last longer than fresh flowers.

# The Courage That My Mother Had

The courage that my mother had
Went with her, and is with her still:
Rock from New England quarried;
 Now granite in a granite hill.

The golden brooch my mother wore
 She left behind for me to wear;
 I have no thing I treasure more:
 Yet, it is something I could spare.

 Oh, if instead she'd left to me
 The thing she took into the grave!
 That courage like a rock, which she
 Has no more need of, and I have.

—Edna St. Vincent Millay

*Mom,*
*I love you to the*
*moon and back.*

# To Read When You're Alone

I was thirteen years old. My family had moved to Southern California from north Florida a year before. I hit adolescence with a vengeance. I was angry and rebellious, with little regard for anything my parents had to say, particularly if it had to do with me. Like so many teenagers, I struggled to escape from anything that didn't agree with my picture of the world. A "brilliant without need of guidance" kid, I rejected any overt offering of love. In fact, I got angry at the mention of the word *love.*

One night, after a particularly difficult day, I stormed into my room, shut the door and got into bed. As I lay down in the privacy of my bed, my hands slipped under my pillow. There was an envelope. I pulled it out and on the envelope it said, "To read when you're alone."

Since I was alone, no one would know whether I read it or not, so I opened it. It said "Mike, I know life is hard right now, I know you are frustrated and I know we don't do everything right. I also know that I love you completely and nothing you do or say will ever change that. I am here for you if you ever need to talk, and if you don't, that's okay. Just know that no matter where you go or what you do in your life, I will always love you and be proud that you are my son. I'm here for you and I love you—that will never change. Love, Mom."

That was the first of several "To read when you're alone" letters. They were never mentioned until I was an adult.

Today I travel the world helping people. I was in Sarasota, Florida, teaching a seminar when, at the end of the day, a lady came up to me and shared the difficulty she was having with her son. We walked out to the beach, and I told her of my mom's undying love and about the "To read when you're alone" letters. Several weeks later, I got a card that said she had written her first letter and left it for her son.

That night as I went to bed, I put my hands under my pillow and remembered the relief I felt every time I got a letter. In the midst of my turbulent teen years, the letters were the calm assurance that I could be loved in spite of me, not because of me. Just before I fell asleep I thanked God that my mom knew what I, an angry teenager, needed. Today when the seas of life get stormy, I know that just under my pillow there is that calm assurance that love—consistent, abiding, unconditional love—changes lives.

*Mike Staver*

(Chicken Soup for the Mother's Soul)

Mom, you have
a special way of
adding happiness
to all the lives
you touch.

*The day the child realizes that all adults are imperfect, he becomes an adolescent; the day he forgives them, he becomes an adult; the day he forgives himself, he becomes wise.*

—Alden Nowlan

# A Mother's
## Mid-Summer Prayer

Dear God,

Grant me the strength to last until Back to School Night.

Give me the energy to drive the swim team carpool, take knots out of wet shoelaces with my teeth and untangle the dog from the sprinkler hose.

Grant me the wisdom to remember the name of the redheaded kid from down the street who hasn't left our house since July.

Walk with me through the backyard over piles of wet bathing suits and empty ice cream cups to rescue my good lipstick from the bottom of the wading pool.

Give me the courage to accept that everything in the refrigerator either has a bite out of it, had a finger stuck in it or is reproducing in the vegetable crisper underneath the expensive cheese.

Guide me down the hallway to the laundry room, where I can experience five minutes of peace and quiet by turning the lights out and climbing on the dryer so the kids can't see my feet underneath the door.

Help me accept the fact that even if I take the kids to the circus, install a pool in the backyard, go on a safari, and carve a redwood tree into a canoe and sail down the Congo, my children will end each day with "I'm bored."

Grant me the serenity to smile when my husband

insists on tossing the Hamburger Helper on the gas grill because "everything tastes better barbecued."

In your infinite wisdom, show me how to disconnect the video game console that hasn't been turned off since June 22.

Comfort me when I realize the color of my earth-tone carpet has changed into a mixture of melted blue Popsicle and the remains of somebody's purple slushie.

And if I ask too much, God, just give me the foresight to know that one day—not too many years from now—the barbecue, television and sprinkler hose will be off; the refrigerator, front door and garage will be closed; and I will wonder where my children—and the little redheaded boy with the glasses—went.

*Debbie Farmer*
(Chicken Soup for the Mother's Soul 2)

53

*Mom,*
*thanks for always*
*loving me . . .*
*even when*
*I wasn't lovable.*

$\mathcal{B}$egin at the beginning and
go on till you come to the end;
then stop.

—Lewis Carroll

## You Know You're a Frazzled Mom If . . .

You forget your kid's name!

You haven't slept eight straight hours in years!

Whenever you go shopping, you hear the familiar voice come over the loud speaker, "Clothes rack over in Ladies."

You look forward to the two days in the hospital after your baby is born . . . just to get some rest!

You have all your kids in bed with you at some point during the night.

You end up screaming, "I have needs too!!" to three stunned faces.

Everyone in the house is screaming your name at the same time.

Your idea of exercising is running around the house in your fuzzy bunny slippers!

Everyone in the store knows the names of your kids by the time you leave!

You deny knowing your kids in public.

You never go to the bathroom alone.

You have no idea what "me time" is.

—Deanne Bland

# *Easy Stain Removal Tips*

**Acrylic paint:** Soak with hairspray
and scrape off the paint.

**Bird droppings:** Allow to dry, then
scrape off as much as possible.
Remove the rest with a weak mixture
of vinegar and water.

**Blood:** Sprinkle liberally with table salt,
rub in and wash.

**Grass stains:** Remove with white vinegar.

**Gum in carpet:** Try lighter fluid or peanut butter!

**Lipstick:** Rub generously with petroleum
jelly, then wash as usual.

**Ring around the collar:**
Wet collar with warm water, sprinkle generously
with cream of tartar and rub in, then wash.

**Tar:** Rub the spot with kerosene, then wash.

**Tea:** Rinse with water, then wash with
lime juice. Launder as usual.

**Wine:** Soak in club soda, then wash in cold water.

# Gotta Watch the Fish Eat

I did something very daring today. I said, "No." I was at a meeting where I was asked to serve on a committee that would require numerous Thursday evening meetings. And I said, "No."

I declined politely, even graciously, but it wasn't enough. The others just looked at me, waiting. Three long seconds, four, five. Waiting, waiting for my important excuse. They couldn't move on until I had explained my answer.

"You see," I continued. "I really want to be home to tuck the kids in bed at night." Most of the others around the table nodded in understanding. "Well," the chairperson offered, "we can make sure we're done by eight-thirty, so you can be home in time to tuck the kids in." The others murmured in affirmation and turned back to me, expectantly, waiting for my response.

"Well," I explained, "that's right when we are watching the fish eat." The others weren't impressed. "You see," I continued, "on Thursdays, after I've quizzed the children for Friday's spelling tests, we watch the fish. It's just an important time in our family's week. It seems to set the tone for the next day, and when I'm gone on Thursday nights, Fridays just don't go as well." My words sounded rather weak and almost silly as they tumbled out. No one said, "Oh, of course, Cheryl, we understand!" They were still waiting.

Now, I could have added, "But, you see, I've got a book manuscript due to the publisher in two months that I have got to work on." That would have been sufficiently important. After all, that's my career. They would have nodded in understanding and quickly moved on. But the truth is, I'm not writing between 7:30 and 8:30 P.M. on Thursday evenings. I'm being Mom. I'm reviewing spelling words for Friday's tests. I'm checking math answers. I'm making sure permission notes are signed, book reports are written and weekly assignments completed. And when school work is done, and the children have brushed their teeth and gotten into their PJs, the family gathers on the couch in front of the aquarium to watch the fish eat. We feed the fish every night, of course. But on Thursdays we make an effort to sit together as a family and watch them. This is when I heard about Blake's plans to be a paleontologist. It's when I learned about how Bryce handled the bully on the playground. This is when Sarah Jean explained why she doesn't want to wear bows in her hair anymore.

The committee members were still looking at me. Feeling guilty, I almost changed my mind to say, "Okay, I'll do it." But I didn't. Because my reason for saying no is important. On Thursday evenings, we watch the fish eat.

*Cheryl Kirking*
(Chicken Soup for Every Mom's Soul)

*59*

*Mom, thanks for always being there for me.*

*W*herever there is a
human being, there is an
opportunity for kindness.

—Seneca

# A Mother Is Born

My first child, a daughter, was born on July 27, 2000, and I found I was completely unprepared. I thought I was ready for her birth. I had read my books and articles on childbirth and baby care; I had bought everything on my shopping checklist. The nursery was ready, and my husband and I were anxiously awaiting her arrival. I was prepared for wakeful nights, endless diapers, sore nipples, crying (both hers and mine) and the feeling that I can't get anything done. I was prepared for sitz baths and hemorrhoids.

What I wasn't prepared for was the way the entire world looked different to me the minute she was born. I wasn't prepared for the fact that the sheer weight of my love for her would reduce me to tears on a daily basis. I didn't know that I wouldn't be able to get through my first lullaby to her because I wouldn't be able to sing through my tears. I didn't know that the world would suddenly become unbelievably beautiful and yet infinitely scarier. I didn't know that it would seem like a new place had been created inside of me just to hold this incredible love.

I had no idea what it would feel like when the nurse wheeled my daughter in to me, saying, "She's looking for you," and the way the image of her deep-blue eyes looking right at me would be seared in my heart forever. I didn't know that I could love someone so much it literally hurts, that a trip to Wal-Mart would make me feel like a protective mother bear guarding her cub or that my first trip to the grocery store without her would break my heart.

I didn't know that she would forever change the way my husband and I look at each other or that the process of giving birth to her and breastfeeding her would give me a whole new respect for my body. No one told me that I would no longer be able to watch the evening news because every story about child abuse would make me think of my daughter's face.

Why didn't anyone warn me about these things? I am over-whelmed by it all. Will I ever be able to leave her and think of anything but her, or see a crust in her eye or spot on her skin that doesn't make me nervous? Will I ever be able to show her and express to her just how deep and all-encompassing my love for her is? Will I ever be able to be the mother I so desper-ately want her to have?

I have heard it said, and I now know that it is true, that when a woman gives birth to her first child, there are two births. The first is the birth of the child. The second is the birth of the mother. Perhaps that is the birth that is impossible to prepare for.

*Regina Phillips*
(Chicken Soup for the Mother and Daughter Soul)

*To love another person is
to see the face of God.*

—Victor Hugo

*Family Time Ideas*

Cook dinner together

Have a family game night

Have "T.V.-Free night"

Bake cookies together

Dance together

Play charades together

Finger paint together

Bike and hike together

Bird watch together

Make sand castles together

Have movie night at home

Tell stories about childhood

Share family traditions from the past

Read together

Plant a garden together

# *The Family Dinner*

I looked at my twin teenagers and wanted to cry. He wore baggy pants, orange hair and earrings. She wore a nose ring, fake tattoo and three-inch nails. It was Passover, and we were on our way to the relatives . . . for dinner . . . to celebrate.

I could just imagine the whispers of their aunts and uncles, the looks, the clucking of tongues and shaking of heads. I could have started an argument right there, at the door, before we left. I could have threatened and ridiculed and grounded. But then what? I knew I didn't want a fight and harsh words on this day.

And so we went. I was ready for the looks, but none came. I was ready for the whispers. None came. My kids sat (looking a bit awkward) around the table of twenty. They sat alongside the scrubbed and perfect shiny faces of their little cousins. They participated in the service, and they sang the holiday songs. My son helped the younger ones read. My daughter helped clear the dishes in between courses. They laughed and joked and helped pour coffee for the elders.

I realized as I watched their beautiful faces that it didn't matter what anyone else thought. Because I thought they were terrific. They were carrying on our tradition with enthusiasm and love. And it was coming naturally—from their hearts.

I knew that the hair, the baggy clothes and fake tattoos were just a statement of who they were for the moment. This would change with time. But their participation in the songs and ceremonies of our holidays and the closeness of our family would be within them always. As they grew older, I knew this would never change.

Soon, the Passover celebration would be over. The loud music, friends and chaos would again be a part of our lives. I didn't want this special night to end. These were precious moments that sneak up on us as mothers. I don't think it matters how young or old our children are. Sometimes, it's just a quick, funny smile or a small gesture they make that sparks that overwhelming feeling of total love.

I watched my son and daughter and felt their peace and happiness. At that moment, I wanted to jump up and hug them. I wanted to tell them what great kids I thought they were. But I didn't. At that moment, I wanted to walk over and pinch their cheeks as I did when they were nine and tell them I thought they were beautiful. But I didn't. Instead, I sat in my place and sang and ate and talked with the others.

Later, on the way home, I would tell them. In private, I would say how much their presence at the table meant to me. I would tell them how great they were and how proud I was to be their mom. Later, when we were alone, I would tell them how much I loved them. And I did.

*Shari Cohen*
(Chicken Soup for the Mother's Soul)

*Mom, you inspire me to be a better person.*

*W*ho takes a child by the
hand, takes the mother by
the heart.

—Danish Proverb

# A Doll from Santa

Alice's mother died when Alice was five years old. Although her nine brothers and sisters were loving and caring, they were no replacement for a mother's love.

The year was 1925, and life was hard. Alice, who grew up to be my mother, told me that her family was too poor to even afford to give her a doll.

In December 1982, I had a job at a local bank. One afternoon, we were decorating the tree in the bank lobby and singing carols, getting ready for the Christmas season. One of my customers approached me with a sample of her handi-work: beautiful handmade dolls. She was taking orders for Christmas. I decided to get one for my daughter, Katie, who was almost five years old. Then I had an idea. I asked my customer if she could make me a special doll for my mother—one with gray hair and spectacles: a grandmother doll.

The doll maker felt that this idea was certainly unique and took it on as a creative challenge. So I placed my Christmas order: two dolls, one blonde and one gray-haired for Christmas morning!

Things really started to fall into place when a friend had told me that his dad—who played Santa Claus at various charitable functions in my area—would be willing to make a visit on Christmas morning to our home to deliver my Katie her presents! Knowing that my parents would be there as well, I began to get ready for what would turn out to be one of the most memorable days of my mother's life.

Christmas Day arrived, and at the planned time, so did Santa Claus. I had prepared the presents for Santa to deliver, along with one for my mother tucked into the bottom of Santa's bag. Katie was surprised and elated that Santa had come to see her at her own house.

My mother was enjoying watching her granddaughter's reaction to the visit from this special guest. As Santa turned to leave, he looked once more into his knapsack and retrieved one more gift. As he asked who Alice was, my mother, taken aback by her name being called, indicated that she, in fact, was Alice. Santa handed her the gift, which was accompanied by a card that read:

For Alice:

I was cleaning out my sleigh before my trip this year and came across this package that was supposed to be delivered on December 25, 1925. The present inside has aged, but I felt that you might still wish to have it. Many apologies for the lateness of the gift.

Love, Santa Claus

My mother's reaction was one of the most profound and deeply emotional scenes I have ever witnessed. She couldn't speak, but only clasped the doll she had waited fifty-seven years to receive as tears of joy coursed down her cheeks. That doll, given by "Santa," made my mother the happiest "child" alive.

*Alice Ferguson*
(Chicken Soup for the Mother's Soul 2)

71

# Mother's Day

Although the first Mother's Day in the United States was established by Julia Ward Howe as an act of pacifism, it was Anna Jarvis, a West Virginia school teacher, who in 1908 heralded Mother's Day as we celebrate it today.

The first Mother's Day of 1908 was celebrated in Grafton, West Virginia, where Anna persuaded her mother's church to commemorate the second anniversary of her mother's death on the second Sunday of May. The church was filled with white carnations, which were Anna's mother's favorites. Since that time, white carnations have been used to commemorate a mother who has passed away, while red carnations are a symbol of a living mother.

# Carnations

Carnations have been cultivated for the past two thousand years and originated in the Near East. The original carnation had a pinkish hue; other colors, like the white and red carnations, only appeared later. Red carnations mean deep love and affection. White carnations mean pure love and good luck.

## Crepe Paper Carnations

INGREDIENTS:

Tissue or crepe paper, a variety of colors
Colored pipe cleaners or twist ties

DIRECTIONS:

Stack 4–6 pieces of crepe or tissue paper together. *(Paper that is 8 by 10 inches is a good size, but you can experiment with different paper to make various flower sizes.)*

Fold the pile of paper like an accordion.

Use the colored pipe cleaner or a twist tie to tie the center of the folded paper.

Gently pull each piece of paper individually toward the top center part of the flower. Make sure you separate each sheet of paper.

Arrange them as you like to make a flower!

*Mom, you're in my thoughts . . . today and always.*

# *It's a Date!*

"Should I meet him there Saturday night?" she asked.

"Of course not. You know the family rule," I said. The cold pork chops hissed against the sizzling skillet. "Your date must always . . ."

"It's *not* a date," she interrupted.

". . . come right to the door," I chanted without missing a beat. We had rehearsed this very conversation before. A slight pause followed. "Where is he taking you?"

"Out for supper and maybe somewhere afterward." Panic peppered her voice. "A whole evening together—alone. What will we talk about?"

"Knowing you, you'll talk about anything and everything. Since when have you been at a loss for words, anyway?" I joked, handing her a short stack of stoneware salad plates.

"But this is different. I hardly know Tom."

Brushing aside crisp kitchen curtains, I peered into the deepening dusk. A gentle rain blurred the boundaries, skewing the scene like a photograph out of focus. "Well, there's always the weather. Better yet, get him to talk about himself. Ask your boyfriend . . ."

"He's *not* my boyfriend."

". . . about his interests. And, by the end of the date . . ."

"It's *not* a date!"

" . . . you'll know each other better and probably have lots to say," I encouraged. After all, I was experienced with this mother-daughter thing. I had raised four teenagers—all at one time—in the not-so-distant past. Could this be much different?

"Well—if you're sure." She paused. "It's just that . . ."

"Yes?" I coaxed, a little impatient with her hesitancy, my mind racing ahead to the details of dinner.

But the voice that answered had slowed, softened and deepened.

"Do you realize how long it's been?" Her words hung there, suspended, unsupported in the sudden silence. Reaching across me to the stove, she flipped the pork chops and turned down the heat.

". . . how long it's been," she cleared her throat, "since I've dated, I mean? Fifty-five years! With your dad gone so long now, I think . . . maybe . . . well . . . maybe it's time. Why, Carol, I was seventeen the last time I went on a date."

I turned—once again a daughter—and winked. "Oh, but Mom . . . it's *not* a date!"

*Carol McAdoo Rehme*
(Chicken Soup for Every Mom's Soul)

## The Most Delicious Pork Chops

INGREDIENTS:

4½-inch-thick pork loin chops
Flour for dredging
1 cup dry breadcrumbs

1 beaten egg
Canola oil
Salt and Pepper

DIRECTIONS:

Place flour and bread crumbs on separate plates and beaten egg in a soup bowl. Salt and pepper the flour. Dredge the pork chops first in the flour, then in the egg and finally in the breadcrumbs.

Place about a ¼ inch of canola in frying pan (enough to cover ½ pork chop).

Heat the oil at medium high for approximately 5 minutes. Oil will be ready when a pinch of bread crumbs from off a pork chop bubbles when dropped in the oil.

Fry the pork chops until deep golden brown on each side. Approximately 2 minutes per side. Remove the pork chops from frying pan to drain on paper towels and salt to taste.

*M*om, *I love you more than dirtbikes.*

—Blake Ryan Oldfield, age 7

# The World's Worst Mother

After mothering me for thirty years, my mom stood in the kitchen of my home and announced these words, "I was the world's worst mother, and I am so sorry." She then proceeded to apologize for all the things that she did wrong in raising me. I realized that she was filled with guilt about the strict rules of her child-raising years, causing me to miss many school dances. She was mortified that she and my father were too poor to afford my high school ring. She was ashamed of herself for punishments that lasted for weeks. She was sad that she tried to choose my friends. My mother went on and on about her mistakes and regrets as tears of pain streamed down her face.

Right at that moment my mom looked so beautiful. I wondered why my entire family, including me, took her for granted. How do you tell your mother all that she is to you? I wanted to tell her that the punishments and strict rules of my childhood have a small spot in my memory in comparison to my recollections of the nights she let me stay up late and bake cookies with her. I kept silent instead of telling her how much it meant that she scraped together the money for my wedding shoes and matching purse. I couldn't swallow the lump in my throat so I could explain all of the millions of ways she makes me feel so special. I should have told my mother, on that day, that of all the people in my life, no one has ever loved me in the unconditional way that she does.

Four years have gone by since the day I didn't tell my mother that her mistakes were tiny molehills, and her love and understanding were big beautiful mountains in my life. But I'm telling her now. Thank you, Mom, and thank you, God, for the world's worst mother.

*Polly Anne Wise*
(Chicken Soup for the Mother and Daughter Soul)

*To regret deeply is to live afresh.*

—Henry David Thoreau

# *Famous TV Moms*

June Cleaver—Leave It to Beaver

Carol Brady—The Brady Bunch

Marion Cunningham—Happy Days

Edith Bunker—All in the Family

Harriet Nelson—Ozzie and Harriet

Peg Bundy—Married . . . with Children

Florida Evans—Good Times

Samantha Stephens—Bewitched

Mama—Mama's Family

Shirley Patridge—The Partridge Family

Morticia Addams—The Addams Family

# Real Vision

My friend Michelle is blind, but you'd never know it. She makes such good use of her other senses, including her "sixth sense" of intuition, that she rarely gives the impression she's missed anything.

Michelle parents her children pretty much like the rest of us, except that she doesn't sweat the small stuff. One area where Michelle rarely argues with her kids is in keeping the house clean. It isn't that Michelle doesn't know when there's a mess. She knows it's time to clean when she steps on crumbs or toys that have been left out. But in Michelle's house, the kids have learned to put their things away because it wouldn't just annoy their mother to have a mess, it could be dangerous for her. Indeed, Michelle moves around her house so fast that often guests don't realize she's blind.

I realized this the first time my six-year-old, Kayla, went to play there. When Kayla came home, she was very excited about her day. She told me they had baked cookies, played games and done art projects. But she was especially excited about her finger-painting project.

"Mom, guess what?" said Kayla, all smiles. "I learned how to mix colors today! Blue and red make purple, and yellow and blue make green! Isn't that neat? And Michelle painted with us. She said she liked the way the paint feels squishing through her fingers."

Something about my child's excitement caught my attention, and I realized that I had never finger-painted with Kayla. I didn't like the mess. As a result, my child had learned about color from a blind friend. The irony made me sit down and take a look at my child and at myself.

Then Kayla said, "Michelle told me my picture showed joy, pride and a sense of accomplishment. She really saw what I was doing!" Kayla said she had never felt how good finger paints felt until Michelle showed her how to paint without looking at her paper.

That's when I realized Kayla didn't know that Michelle was blind. It had just never come up in conversation.

When I told her, she was quiet for a moment. At first, she didn't believe me. "But Mommy, Michelle understood exactly what was in my picture!" Kayla insisted. And I knew my child was right because Michelle had listened to Kayla describe her artwork. Michelle had also heard Kayla's pride in her work, her wonder at her discovery of the way colors blend and her delight in the texture of the medium.

We were silent for a minute. Then Kayla said slowly, "You know, Mommy, Michelle really did 'see' my picture. She just used my eyes."

I've never heard anyone refer to Michelle as handicapped. She isn't. Hers is a special type of "vision" that all mothers could use.

*Marsha Arons*
(Chicken Soup for the Mother's Soul)

# The Mother

There will be a singing in your heart,
There will be a rapture in your eyes;
You will be a woman set apart,
You will be so wonderful and wise.
You will sleep, and when from dreams you start,
As of one that wakes in Paradise,
There will be a singing in your heart,
There will be a rapture in your eyes.

There will be a moaning in your heart,
There will be an anguish in your eyes,
You will see your dearest ones depart,
You will hear their quivering good-byes.
You will be the heart-ache and the smart,
Tears that scald and lonely sacrifice;
There will be a moaning in your heart,
There will be an anguish in your eyes.

There will come a glory in your eyes,
There will come a peace within your heart;
Singing 'neath the quiet evening skies,
Time will dry the tear and dull the smart.
You will know that you have played your part,
You shall be the love that never dies:
You, with Heaven's peace within your heart,
You, with God's own glory in your eyes.

—Robert Service

# Mama's Medicines

Mama never got close to a medical school, but she had innovative ideas about doctoring. Having seven children and living nine miles away from a doctor called for creativity. Many times I feigned wellness so I wouldn't have to take her cures. Whatever the ailment, she always said, "Take something to clean you out."

Mama kept her medicines on the first shelf of the cabinet, always convenient and in sight. A prescription for springtime blahs was black draught tea, brewed, strained and lukewarm. It looked black and ugly. It tasted black and ugly. Once she added a spoon of sugar, but that did not help. The gold and black box of tea was a regular medication in the cabinet.

Mama finally gave up on giving me castor oil. She thought it was the wonder drug of the ages and presented a gagging spoonful for any occasion. But it was slick and slimy and nearly always came back up. She stopped buying Pepto-Bismol after I drank a full bottle because it was pretty and pink and tasted good. To this day, I don't drink anything pink and thick.

For the flu, Mama's favorite medicine was Carter's Little Liver Pills. They were small and powerful beyond imagination. Mama said the liver was the most important organ in my body and caused all the other parts to operate. With a glass of water, the pills went down easier than castor oil.

Mama had cures for the outsides as well as the insides. If I stepped on a rusty nail or scratched myself climbing a barbed-wire fence, the wound was treated with coal oil, called kerosene these days. The odor and fumes were so strong those germs had to suffocate when the coal oil hit them.

A disgraceful disease was the itch, called seven-year itch by kids at school, though it didn't last seven years, just about seven days with treatment. "Nice people" didn't get the itch, but we got it. As the school year drew to a close, my two sisters and I found ourselves scratching little red bumps. We were glad school was out and no one would know we had the itch. The treatment was horrendous. Each day we mixed yellow sulfur powder with lard and rubbed it on our bodies wherever the itch appeared. Despite the bad smell, the sulfur and lard cured the itch.

Years later when I served in the U.S. Navy, I learned the itch had a real name—scabies. I don't know how the navy treated scabies, but I bet it was not as disagreeable as the way Mama fought it.

A recent bout of bronchitis sent me to the doctor for a chest X-ray and two prescriptions, costing $107.83. Mama would have prescribed Vick's salve rubbed on my chest with a flannel rag to cover it and, of course, Carter's Little Liver Pills to clean me out.

Perhaps Mama's medicines helped me survive. I certainly survived her medicines. She's gone now, and I miss her. Strangely, I miss her most of all when I am sick.

*Lee Hill-Nelson*

(Chicken Soup for the Golden Soul)

## *Mom's Home Remedies*

**Nausea:** Drink ginger tea or
suck on ginger candy

**Pimple:** Dab with regular *(not gel)* toothpaste

**Bad breath:** Chew parsley leaves

**Bruise:** Slice a raw onion and place over bruise,
or apply the inside of a ripe banana peel to
the bruise and keep on overnight

**Insect bite:** Make a paste of cornstarch
and water and apply

**Stinky feet:** Soak your feet in warm *(not hot!)*
tea every night until the problem is gone

**Wart:** Apply duct tape; change daily until it's gone

**Leg cramp:** Place a spoon against the
cramp and it will disappear

**Common cold:** Eat chicken soup, of course!

*Mom, your smiles are the sunshine in my life.*

# Next to My Heart

The day I had to stop dead in my tracks in the aisle of a busy supermarket was one of the worst in my whole life.

There I was, pregnant as could be—forty pounds overweight, a whole month past my due date, with wretched "morning sickness" that lasted twenty-four hours every single day. And now I had cramps in both feet so excruciating I couldn't move.

This wasn't the way I had expected motherhood to be. My own mother, who had six children, glowed when she was expecting. And her mother, my grandmother, not only joyfully welcomed sixteen little ones into the world—but also ran a busy store the entire time.

An office-mate with the same due date as me worked right up till her baby came. My next-door neighbor had done everything she wanted to for nine full months while looking absolutely gorgeous. Neither had been ill a minute.

Meanwhile, I was still pregnant, still miserable, and so large I had long since forgotten what either my feet or my legs looked like. There was only one outfit I could even get on—a sort of muumuu tent.

And now during one of the hottest Augusts on record, my ankles swelled so badly in our sweltering apartment, I had to keep them in buckets of ice. Going anywhere was torture. But we were out of milk. Just a quick dash to the store, I thought—surely I could do that.

So here I was, frozen in my tracks, stopping carts in both directions.

My face beet-red, I stared at the rows of cracker boxes in front of me, pretending not to notice the angry shoppers whose way I was blocking. And then I heard a little girl's voice: "Mommy, why does that lady look so funny?"

I squeezed my eyes shut, trying to stop sudden tears. *Oh, God, please! Can't anyone say anything nice about me for a change? Won't I ever be normal and comfortable and well again? Won't I ever get to hold this baby in my arms?*

Then that mother said something I will never forget: "Dear," she murmured, "it's because God has given that woman a tiny baby to carry next to her heart."

When I opened my eyes, mother and daughter were gone. Eventually, so were the cramps. But those words have lasted a lifetime.

For, oh, they were so true. And such a blessing to me during those final miserable days before I did hold my beautiful first-born in my arms. During my next two pregnancies as well. A blessing I remembered as my three children grew up and married. A blessing I have been privileged to share with my own pregnant daughters-in-law and many other young women I have known over the years.

For even after our children are born, we mothers still carry those precious little ones next to our hearts. And we will our whole lives long.

*Bonnie Compton Hanson*
(Chicken Soup for the Mother's Soul 2)

*Mom, you make me feel as warm as sunlight spilling through an open window.*

*The heart of a mother is a deep abyss at the bottom of which you will always find forgiveness.*

—Honoré de Balzac

# *An Impromptu Dance at Dusk*

Engrossed at the computer, I was typing some very impassioned poetry written by my eighty-two-year-old neighbor, Rosemary. My six-year-old son, Jake, ran up to me. "Mom, let's do something fun together. Now! C'mon!"

Deeply engrossed in the stories of Rosemary's unfulfilled dreams and missed opportunities, I was ready to reply, "Jake, we'll do something in a little bit. I want to work a little longer." Instead, Rosemary's words haunted me, carrying new meaning in my own life. I thought of her sad laments. The wisdom of her years spoke to me, and I decided the poems could wait. My son could not.

"What would you like to do?" I asked, thinking of the new library books we could read together.

"Let's dance," he replied.

"Dance?" I asked.

"Yes, just you and me . . . pleeeeez; I'll be right back," he said as he dashed out of the room. He returned a few moments later with his hair a bit wet and combed over to the side, a shy smile and his black, flowing Batman-turned-into-Prince-Jake cape over his shoulders. He pulled me off my chair and led me upstairs.

The blinds were up and the descending sun was casting shadows against the picturesque night sky. Jake led me to the middle of his braided wool rug and then turned on the radio. "There, Mom. I found us some rock and roll." He took my hand, and we danced, twisted, turned and twirled. We giggled and laughed and danced some more.

My side aching, I told him I needed a rest. Ever so seriously he responded, "Mom, let me put something romantic on now." He found a beautiful slow song, bowed and then took my hand as we began to slow dance together. His head was at my waist, but our feet kept rhythmic time.

"Mom," he said a moment later as he looked up at me, "can you get down on your knees and dance with me so we can look at each other's face while we dance?" I almost responded with why I wouldn't be able to comply with his ridiculous request. Instead, captured by the moment, I laughed, dropped down on my knees, and my little man led me in a dance I will always cherish.

Jake looked deep into my eyes and claimed, "You're my darling, Mom. I'll always love you forever and ever." I thought of the few short years I had left before an obvious list of my faults would replace Jake's little-boy idolization. Of course, he would still love me—but his eyes would lose some of the innocence and reverence they now revealed.

"Mommy," he said. "We'll always be together. Even when one of us dies, we'll always be together in our hearts."

"Yes, we will, Jake. We'll always be together no matter what," I whispered as I wiped a silent tear.

Dusk quietly settled in as this Mom and her Little Prince danced together, ever so slowly, cheek to cheek . . . and heart to heart.

*Marian Gormley*
(Chicken Soup for Every Mom's Soul)

*Patience is the mother of
a beautiful child.*

—Bantu Proverb

*Mom, I wish you everything that will make your heart as happy as you've made mine.*

# A Second Chance

I grew up as a foster child from the age of eight. Unlike most children I knew, I never really had a biological mother. I never got to experience the unconditional love and wonderment a mother gives her child. So growing up was a bit harder on me than on most other children. A drastic change came suddenly when I was in the eleventh grade. I was now in my second foster home and had been there for the past five years. I was surrounded by a warm and caring family. But still something pained me deeply. I felt "out of place." I wasn't my foster mother's birth child, so I remained distant, not allowing myself to love her as much as I could.

In one night, things changed for the better and forever. I was doing homework while waiting for the rest of the family to return home from their events. It was a daily routine. I spent most of my nights by myself finding things to keep me busy. As I was reading a paragraph for English, I heard the closing of the back door and my foster mom calling for me. I walked into the kitchen where she was holding a hardcover children's book that she had borrowed from work. "I want you to read this," she said excitedly. "It's absolutely wonderful." She handed me the book, and I glanced at it with curiosity: *The Kissing Hand* by Audrey Penn. I was just about to question her when she smiled at me. "Trust me. You'll love it!"

Reluctantly, I grabbed a stool, made myself comfortable

at the counter and began to read the book. I thoroughly enjoyed it. It was a touching story of a raccoon mom who places a kiss in the palm of her child's hand to remind him that if ever he should get scared he just has to press his Kissing Hand to his cheek. That way he can always remember that his mommy loves him. I wondered why my foster mom asked me to read it. But I shrugged off the unknown answer and headed back to my room to complete my unfinished homework.

Later that night, I was sitting at the same spot where I had read the book and talking with Mom when suddenly she did something totally unexpected. She ever so gently took my hand and put a warm, loving kiss in the center of my palm. She then quietly closed my hand and held it between hers and spoke words that I had dreamt of hearing for so long. "Whenever you get scared or sad, remember that your mommy loves you."

As the tears began to form in my eyes, I began to understand, and so I smiled a smile that touched the very depth of my once-wounded heart. I truly do have a mother. No, she wasn't biological, but she was mine just the same.

*Cynthia Blatchford*
(Chicken Soup for the Mother and Daughter Soul)

*Mom, you make the world beautiful.*

*In search of my mother's garden, I found my own.*

—Alice Walker

*Chester felt his mother's kiss rush from his hand, up his arm, and into his heart.*

—from *The Kissing Hand,*
by Audrey Penn

# My Mother's Kiss

My mother's kiss, my mother's kiss,
I feel its impress now;
As in the bright and happy days
She pressed it on my brow.

You say it is a fancied thing
Within my memory fraught;
To me it has a sacred place—
The treasure house of thought.

Again, I feel her fingers glide
Amid my clustering hair;
I see the love-light in her eyes,
When all my life was fair.

Again, I hear her gentle voice
In warning or in love.
How precious was the faith that taught
My soul of things above.

—Frances Ellen Watkins Harper

# My Daughter, My Teacher

Children teach us something every day. As a parent, I have learned to expect this. Yet sometimes the extent of what my daughter teaches surprises me.

When Marissa was six months old, it seemed she was always looking up. As I gazed upward with her, I learned the magic of leaves dancing on trees and the awesome size of the tail of a jet. At eight months she was forever looking down. I learned that each stone is different, sidewalk cracks make intricate designs and blades of grass come in a variety of greens.

Then she turned eleven months and began saying "Wow!" She spoke this marvelous word for anything new and wonderful to her, such as the assortment of toys she spotted in the pediatrician's office or the gathering of clouds before a storm. She whispered, "Oh, wow!" for things that really impressed her, like a brisk breeze on her face or a flock of geese honking overhead. Then there was the ultimate in "Wow," a mouthing of the word with no sound, reserved for truly awesome events. These included the sunset on a lake after a magnificent day in Minnesota and fireworks in the summer sky.

She has taught me many ways to say "I love you." She said it well one morning when she was fourteen months old. We were cuddling. She buried her head in my shoulder and, with a sigh of contentment, said "Happy." Another day (during her terrific twos), she pointed to a beautiful model on the cover of a magazine and said, "Is that you, Mom?" Most recently my now three-year-old walked into the kitchen while I was cleaning up after supper and said, "Can I help?" Shortly after this she put her hand on my arm and said, "Mom, if you were a kid, we'd be friends."

At moments like this, all I can say is, "Oh, wow!"

*Janet S. Meyer*
(Chicken Soup for the Mother's Soul)

*Children share with geniuses an open, inquiring, uninhibited quality of mind.*

—Chauncey Guy Suits

Mom, I love you
because you let
me find my
own way.

## How do I love thee?
## Let me count the ways.

I love thee to the depth and breadth and height

My soul can reach, when feeling out of sight

For the ends of Being and ideal Grace.

I love thee to the level of everyday's

Most quiet need, by sun and candle-light.

I love thee freely, as men strive for Right;

I love thee purely, as they turn from Praise.

I love thee with a passion put to use

In my old griefs, and with my childhood's faith.

I love thee with a love I seemed to lose

With my lost saints,—I love thee with the breath,

Smiles, tears, of all my life!—and, if God choose,

I shall but love thee better after death.

—Elizabeth Barrett Browning

# *A World of Love*

Ti voglio bene (Italian)

Ich liebe dich (German)

Je t'aime (French)

Wo ie ni (Chinese)

Te amo (Spanish)

Volim te (Croatian)

Eu te amo (Protuguese)

Miluji te (Czech)

Jeg elsker dig (Danish)

S' agapo (Greek)

Ta gra agam ort (Gaelic)

Seni seviyorum (Turkish)

Szeretlek te'ged (Hungarian)

Ikh hob dikh lib (Yiddish)

Kimi o ai shiteru (Japanese)

# Mothers and Daughters

"You won't forget to bring the potato masher, will you?" I said to my mother on the phone after telling her I had to have a mastectomy. Even at eighty-two and three thousand miles away on the long-distance line, she knew what I meant: soupy mashed potatoes.

This was what she had made for every illness or mishap of my childhood—served in a soup bowl with a nice round spoon. But I had been lucky as a child and was rarely sick. Most often the potato medicine soothed disappointment or nourished a mild cold. This time I was seriously ill.

Arriving on the midnight plane from Virginia, Mom looked fresh as a daisy when she walked through the front door of my house in California the day after I came home from the hospital. I could barely keep my eyes open, but the last thing I saw before I fell asleep was Mom unzipping her carefully packed suitcase and taking out her sixty-year-old potato masher. The one she received as a shower gift, the one with the worn wooden handle and the years of memories.

She was mashing potatoes in my kitchen the day I told her tearfully that I would have to undergo chemotherapy. She put the masher down and looked me squarely in the eye. "I'll stay with you, however long it takes," she told me. "There is nothing more important I have to do in my life than help you get well." I had always thought I was the stubborn one in my family, but in the five months that followed I saw that I came by my trait honestly.

Mom had decided that I would not predecease her. She simply would not have it. She took me on daily walks even when I couldn't get any farther than our driveway. She crushed the pills I had to take and put them in jam, because even in middle age, with a grown daughter of my own, I couldn't swallow pills any better than when I was a child.

When my hair started to fall out, she bought me cute hats. She gave me warm ginger ale in a crystal wineglass to calm my tummy and sat up with me on sleepless nights. She served me tea in china cups.

When I was down, she was up. When she was down, I must have been asleep. She never let me see it. And, in the end, I got well. I went back to my writing.

I have discovered that Mother's Day doesn't happen some Sunday in May, but on every day you are lucky enough to have a mother around to love you.

*Patricia Bunin*

(Chicken Soup for the Mother's Soul 2)

## *Yummy Mashed Potatoes*

INGREDIENTS:

2½ pounds of baking potatoes
¾ cup milk
½ stick of butter
1 teaspoon salt
¼ teaspoon black pepper
Pinch of freshly grated nutmeg

DIRECTIONS:

Cut potatoes into 1-inch chunks. Put the potatoes in a 4-quart saucepan and cover with cold water. Bring potatoes to a boil and cook for 20 minutes, or until potatoes are tender. Drain the potatoes well and return them to the saucepan. Add the butter and break the potatoes up with a potato masher. Add half the milk and incorporate while mashing and stirring. Continue to add milk in small batches until the potatoes are smooth and satiny. Do not overwork the potatoes.

Serves 4 to 6 people.

*They must often change,
who would be constant in
happiness or wisdom.*

—Confucius

# *Anticipating the Empty Nest*

Tomorrow is about to arrive. My first child is preparing to leave for college, and the family unit will change forever. This is not a surprise to me, and yet, I am deeply surprised by how quickly this day is speeding toward us. I'm not quite finished with her. I feel betrayed by time.

This is a happy and healthy step in the expected, and hoped for, chain of milestones. She is eager and ready to leave, but I am not nearly ready to let her go. I need to make a few more cupcakes with her, read and recite from *Goodnight Moon,* and maybe create one more fruit basket from Play-Doh. I want to tell her, "Wait a minute!" and have her stand still. And in that time I would hurry to fill her head with the things about life that I am afraid I forgot to tell her. But standing still, she would impatiently reply, "Yes, Mom, I know. You've told me." And she would be right, but I can't help feeling that I forgot something.

Seventeen years ago, as I stood over her crib watching her breathe, I wrote a letter to my four-day-old infant. It said, "These are the days when doorknobs are unreachable, the summer is long and tomorrow takes forever to arrive." In this letter I told her of the plans and dreams I had for the two of us. I promised her tea parties in winter and tents in the spring. We would do art projects and make surprises for her daddy. We would examine sand and flowers and rocks and snowflakes. We would smell the grass, the ocean and burning wood.

We experienced so much more than I promised on that night long ago. We endured many of life's painful interruptions. When the continuity of our plans had to pause to accommodate sorrow, we grew from the shared hurt and the coping. I never promised her that all of our experiences would be happy, just that her father and I would be there with unquestioning support.

When this tomorrow is actually here, I will keep the final promise I made to my baby daughter. In the letter I told her, "I will guide you as safely as I can to the threshold of adulthood; and there, I will let you go . . . for the days quickly pass when doorknobs are unreachable, summers are long and tomorrow takes forever to arrive."

As I prepare to let her go, I reflect upon her first day of nursery school, when I, like countless mothers before me, said good-bye to a tearful child and went back to look in the school window a few minutes later. I needed to know if she was still crying. I believe that when I leave this child at her college dorm, she will slip down to the parking lot and find me there, crying.

Seventeen years ago I watched her breathe. Tomorrow I will watch her fly.

*Bonnie Feuer*
(Chicken Soup for Every Mom's Soul)

## Tips for Coping with Empty Nest Syndrome

• Do something for yourself that you've been putting off: take a class or a trip, start a hobby, plant a garden, read all the books you never had time to read!

• Rekindle your romance with your spouse or significant other. Go out to dinner, go away for a long weekend, take a class as a couple.

• If the kids are gone for good, plan something new for the empty bedroom(s). Make an office or sitting room for yourself. Redecorate it as the guest bedroom you never had!

• Send goody bags to your kids to let them know you are still interested in their lives. E-mail or call them—but in moderation.

• Rekindle your friendships. Form relationships with other "empty-nesting" couples or friends. Invite your friends to coffee or shopping.

• Adopt a loveable cat or dog to care for.

• Now's the time to pursue your dreams: start your own business; write that novel you've always wanted to write; sign up for college classes.

*Mom, I love you because you believe in me . . . always.*

*Youth fades, love droops,
the leaves of friendship fall.
A mother's secret hope out-
lives them all.*

—Oliver Wendell Holmes

## *The World of Mothers*

Mere, Maman (French)

Mutter, Mutti (German)

Maji (Hindi)

Madre, Mamma (Italian)

Mãe (Portuguese)

Majka (Serbian)

Abatyse (Czech)

Moeder; Moer (Dutch)

Ema (Estonian)

Màna (Greek)

Anya, Fu (Hungarian)

Madre (Spanish)

Mor (Norwegian)

# *More Than*
# *a Pair of Gloves*

Albert Einstein once said, "Only a life lived for others is a life worthwhile." These words eloquently describe all that my mother was. She loved and gave unselfishly, despite turmoil in her own life. Struggling to maintain a marriage to an alcoholic and to raise four daughters practically on her own, she still found time to give to others. Life was never easy, but our home was filled as much with laughter and fun as it was with tears, if not more. She passed this love of life, laughter and people on to her daughters and grandchildren.

I recall an incident in grade school when Mom noticed my classmate and her siblings did not have any mittens, hats or scarves. The next day, a package was on the desk of each of the six kids, containing two hats, two sets of gloves and two scarves. I can't forget the joy in my classmate's eyes upon receiving such a simple gift and the pride with which she and her siblings wore them. It seemed like such a simple gift but meant the world to those kids.

Mom bought those gifts without thinking twice. She told me it was because when she was a child, she and her siblings were always the ones with the flimsy jackets in the cold winter and with chapped, gloveless hands. No one helped them. She couldn't bear to think of that happening to any more kids.

Whenever I see a child without a jacket or gloves, I

don't see a stranger; I see my mother, aunts and uncles. That is what she taught me to see: It may not be you or a loved one right now, but it may have been you yesterday and could be you tomorrow. Use your knowledge and experience to make a difference in someone's life. This difference can be as simple as a pair of gloves.

In 1990, my mother's life was cut short by the selfishness of a drunk driver. I was sixteen and had so much left to learn from Mom, but she had already taught me her greatest lesson— loving and caring unselfishly.

I've always realized how important my mother was to our family, but it has taken seven years since her death to learn what she meant to others. Recently, I received a letter from a long-time family friend. It told me so much I already knew about Mom but never knew others had seen in her, too. This friend told me she thinks of Mom almost every day and will never be able to put into words how thankful she is for having known my mother.

This is perhaps the greatest gift I have ever received, knowing that my mother wasn't a gift only to me, but was precious to everyone who was blessed to have known her. It was a pair of gloves, but it was my mother's own simple gift to me.

*Julia Alene Doyle*
(Chicken Soup for the Mother and Daughter Soul)

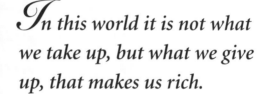

*In this world it is not what we take up, but what we give up, that makes us rich.*

—Henry Ward Beecher

*Mom, you are
a special blessing
to me.*

# Dance with Me

When we're young and we dream of love and fulfill-ment, we think perhaps of moon-drenched Parisian nights or walks along the beach at sunset.

No one tells us that the greatest moments of a life-time are fleeting, unplanned and nearly always catch us off guard.

Not long ago, as I was reading a bedtime story to my seven-year-old daughter, Annie, I became aware of her focused gaze. She was staring at me with a far-away, trancelike expression. Apparently, completing *The Tale of Samuel Whiskers* was not as important as we first thought.

I asked what she was thinking about.

"Mommy," she whispered, "I just can't stop looking at your pretty face."

I almost dissolved on the spot.

Little did she know how many trying moments the glow of her sincerely loving statement would carry me through over the following years.

Not long after, I took my four-year-old son to an elegant department store, where the melodic notes of a classic love song drew us toward a tuxedoed musician playing a grand piano. Sam and I sat down on a marble bench nearby, and he seemed as transfixed by the lilting theme as I was.

I didn't realize that Sam had stood up next to me until he turned, took my face in his little hands and said, "Dance with me."

If only those women strolling under the Paris moon knew the joy of such an invitation made by a round-cheeked boy with baby teeth. Although shoppers openly chuckled, grinned and pointed at us as we glided and whirled around the open atrium, I would not have traded a dance with such a charming young gentleman if I'd been offered the universe.

*Jean Harper*
(Chicken Soup for the Mother's Soul)

*Once upon a time there was an old cat, called Mrs. Tabitha Twitchit, who was an anxious parent. She used to lose her kittens continually, and whenever they were lost they were always in mischief!*

—Excerpted from *The Tale of Samuel Whiskers*, by Beatrix Potter, originally published in 1908

*Mom, thinking
of you always
gives my heart
a lift!*

# *About the Authors*

## Who Is Jack Canfield?

**Jack Canfield** is one of America's leading experts in the development of human potential and personal effectiveness. He is both a dynamic, entertaining speaker and a highly sought-after trainer. Jack has a wonderful ability to inform and inspire audiences toward increased levels of self-esteem and peak performance. He has authored or coauthored numerous books, including *Dare to Win, The Aladdin Factor, 100 Ways to Build Self-Concept in the Classroom, Heart at Work* and *The Power of Focus.* His latest book is *The Success Principles.*

*www.jackcanfield.com*

## Who is Mark Victor Hansen?

In the area of human potential, no one is more respected than **Mark Victor Hansen**. For more than thirty years, Mark has focused solely on helping people from all walks of life reshape their personal vision of what's possible. His powerful messages of possibility, opportunity and action have created powerful change in thousands of organizations and millions of individuals worldwide. He is a prolific writer of bestselling books such as *The One Minute Millionaire, The Power of Focus, The Aladdin Factor* and *Dare to Win.*

*www.markvictorhansen.com*

# Contributors

**Marsha Arons** is a writer and speaker. Her areas of interest include women's issues, child-parent relationships, Christian-Jewish relations and focusing on the positive aspects of life. She is delighted to be a contributor to numerous *Chicken Soup* books. In addition, Marsha's stories, essays and articles have appeared in *Good Housekeeping, Redbook, Woman's Day, Woman's World* and *Reader's Digest*. She is currently at work on a collection of stories having to do with parenting and on a novel for young adults. She can be reached for writing and speaking assignments at *ra8737@aol.com* or by calling 847-329-0280.

**Julie Bete** lives the good life in southern Vermont. She spends her days playing Simon Says, dancing with fairies and breastfeeding the unquenchable nursling. She enjoys gardening, reading, writing, plant spirit medicine, local organic produce and giving birth at home. Her husband and daughter bring laughter to her days.

**Deanne Bland** is the proud, frazzled mom of three wonderful boys who keep life very interesting. She is happily married to her soulmate, Richard, active in her church, and in her "spare" time maintains her Web sites *www.frazzledmom.com* and *www.kinfolkcrafts.com*. Contact Deanne at *bland@kinfolkcrafts.com*.

**Cynthia Blatchford** is an aspiring writer with profound hopes of helping others heal through the written word based on her life's experiences. Her interests include reading, crafts and a vast love of movies. She may be reached by e-mail at *cindy_700@hotmail.com*.

**Patricia Bunin** is a writer and breast cancer survivor from Altadena, California. She writes regularly for the *Pasadena Star News* and is working on an inspirational book about her experience with cancer. She is available for freelance writing assignments or speaking engagements. You can reach her at 626-797-8255 or e-mail her at *patriciabunin@ix.netcom.com.*

**Kristina Cliff-Evans** is in her third and favorite career—writing. With many publication credits and several writing awards, Kristina currently writes for children and has completed her first novel. She and her husband, an architect, have three grown children. She can be reached via e-mail at *tinaeva@compaq.net.*

**Shari Cohen** is the author of eight books for children. She also writes articles for magazines and newspapers about family life. Shari lives in Woodland Hills, California, with her husband, Paul, and their three teenagers. She can be reached at P.O. Box 6593, Woodland Hills, CA 91365.

**Julia Alene Doyle** is an aspiring writer and photographer. A native of Waukegan, Illinois, she lives in Alexandria, Indiana, and is employed by the newspaper industry. Her passage is dedicated to her nieces and nephews, who remain a constant source of pride and inspiration. She can be reached at *jules_274@hotmail.com.*

**Karen C. Driscoll** lives with her husband and their four children in Connecticut. Her work has been published in *Woman's World, Brain, Child, Chicken Soup for the Soul, Chocolate for a Woman's Soul, Angels on Earth, Mothering Magazine* and the anthology *Toddler.* She can be reached at *kmhbdriscoll@hotmail.com.*

**Debbie Farmer** is a nationally syndicated humor columnist. Her column "Family Daze" is distributed by Paradigm TSA Syndicate (*www.paradigm-tsa.com*). Her column has been internationally published in parenting magazines in the United States, Canada and Australia. Her essays have also appeared nationally in Disney's *Family Fun Magazine, Christian Parenting Today* and Sunset Publications Specialty Magazines. Visit her Web site at *www.familydaze.com.*

**Alice Ferguson** was born and raised in Derry, New Hampshire, and currently resides in Reno, Nevada. Alice holds a master's degree in liberal arts and teaches English composition at the University of Nevada/Reno. When not teaching, Alice divides her time between travel in her RV and spending time with her two children.

**Bonnie Feuer** had her own column ("Wisdom and Warmth") in several newspapers and was published in *Better Health Magazine*. She won *Better Health*'s Writer of the Year with her story, "Silver Linings." Employed by the board of education, she is currently writing an interactive book for children.

**Marian Gormley** is a freelance writer and photographer whose work has appeared in regional and national publications. She has a background in software engineering, public relations and marketing. She enjoys writing about issues related to parenting and family life, education, and health. Marian resides in northern Virginia with her husband and twin children.

**Bonnie Compton Hanson,** editor, artist and author, is also represented in *Chicken Soup for the Pet Lover's Soul.* Her lively family includes husband, Don, children, grandchildren, birds, cats and possums. You may reach Bonnie at 3330 S. Lowell St., Santa Ana, CA 92707; phone: 714-751-7824; e-mail: *bonnieh1@worldnet. att.net.*

**Jean Harper** is a wife, mother of two, writer, public speaker and pilot for United Airlines, currently a captain on the Boeing 757. She considers her finest talent to be storytelling and uses her varied and unusual background in public speaking to address the subjects of aviation, Christianity and career guidance, as well as inspirational topics.

**Lee Hill-Nelson** is a wife, mother, grandmother and retired church secretary. She began writing in 1986 when her children asked her to record her memories about growing up. She has been published in several newspapers and magazines.

In a former life, **Peggy Jaeger** was a registered nurse who always yearned to write. After the birth of her daughter, she became a full-time wife, mother and author. She's had numerous fiction short stories and nursing articles published and is currently working on a mystery-suspense novel.

**Kendeyl Johansen** is an award-winning author and contributing editor for iParenting Media and the national magazines *Pregnancy, Woman's Health & Fitness* and *Baby Years.* Her work has also appeared in *Woman's World* and several literary journals. You may contact her at *larsken@burgoyne.com.*

**Vicki Marsh Kabat** received her bachelor of arts in journalism from the University of Missouri at Columbia. She is editor of *Baylor Magazine* for Baylor University in Waco, Texas. For ten years, she wrote a newspaper humor column that was distributed nationally. Her work appeared in *Chicken Soup for the Golden Soul.* She and her husband, Bruce, have three grown sons: Michael, Jeffrey and Brian. Please e-mail her at *Vicki_Marsh-Kabat@baylor.edu.*

**Cheryl Kirking** is the author of *Crayons in the Dryer: Misadventures and Unexpected Blessings of Motherhood.* She is a women's conference speaker who tickles the funny bones and tugs at the heartstrings of audiences nationwide. She has written five books, including *Ripples of Joy* and *Teacher, You're an A+,* and is the mother of teenage triplets! For booking information, visit *www.cherylkirking.com.*

**Jeanette Lisefski** is the proud mother of three fantastic children and the founder of At-Home Mothers' Resource Center and the National Association of At-Home Mothers. These organizations provide mothers-at-home, and those who want to be, with a wide array of information, services, support and encouragement to help make at-home motherhood work for them. You can reach Jeanette at At-Home Mothers' Resource Center, 406 E. Buchanan, Fairfield, IA 52556 or fax her at 515-469-3068; e-mail *ahmrc@lisco.com*.

**Janet S. Meyer** is a writer and therapist in La Crosse, Wisconsin. She lives with her husband, Gerry, daughter, Melissa, and keeshond, Kudos. Her passions include parenting, pets and travel. Motherhood continues to amaze and inspire her.

**Caurie Anne Miner** is the daughter of Dawn and Gregory Miner and sister of Stephanie, K. T. and Christopher. Caurie—a freelance writer—was raised on the family's tree farm in upstate New York. She earned her bachelor's and master's degrees from the University of Rochester and is a former Fulbright Grant recipient. Caurie's mom recently graduated from Green Mountain College with her "official" teaching credentials. You can reach them both at 217 Scotch Hill Road, Cambridge, NY 12816 or *caurieanne@hotmail.com*.

**Regina Phillips** holds a bachelor's degree in social work and currently works for a legal information service company. She lives in Columbus, Ohio, with her husband and their daughter. She can be reached by e-mail at *ginamp1976@yahoo.com*.

**Carol McAdoo Rehme,** one of *Chicken Soup's* most prolific contributors, recognizes motherhood as her most important calling—it keeps her humble and hopping. She is "Mom" to four plus two sons-in-love. Carol directs a nonprofit, Vintage Voices, Inc., which brings interactive programming to the vulnerable elderly. Contact her at *carol@rehme.com; www.rehme.com*.

**Sallie Rodman** is a freelance writer residing in Los Alamitos, California, with her husband, a dog and a cat. She has a certificate in professional writing from California State University, Long Beach. Her work has appeared in *Chocolate for a Woman's Courage, Byline, The Mystery Review* and *Good Dog!* She enjoys writing about the synchronicity of life in everyday events. E-mail her at *srodman@ix.netcom.com*.

**Michael L. Staver** is a motivational speaker/consultant and personal coach. He is passionately committed to encouraging people to pursue their dreams. When he is not on the road, he lives in California. He can be reached at 714-741-3012.

**Polly Anne Wise** was born in Baltimore, Maryland, to Paul and Betty White in June 1964. She currently resides in Westminster, Maryland. Polly is the mother of two: Jeffrey Scott and Samantha Nicole. She now works as general manager of a convenience store chain, Jiffy Mart. She also is a cheerleading coach, and her team has been National Champions for the past three years.

## Permissions

*Motherhood: A Transformation.* Reprinted by permission of Margaret-Mary Jaeger. ©1996 Margaret-Mary Jaeger.

*The Baby Book.* Reprinted by permission of Julie Bete. ©2001 Julie Bete.

*Lessons on Napkins.* Reprinted by permission of Caurie Anne Miner. ©1999 Caurie Anne Miner.

*Mother's Lessons Can Last a Lifetime.* Reprinted by permission of Vicki Marsh Kabat. ©1999 Vicki Marsh Kabat.

*The Rocker.* Reprinted by permission of Kendeyl Johansen. ©1998 Kendeyl Johansen.

*Forever, for Always and No Matter What!* Reprinted by permission of Jeanette Lisefski. ©1997 Jeanette Lisefski.

*The Mirror Has Three Faces.* Reprinted by permission of Kristina Cliff-Evans. ©1999 Kristina Cliff-Evans.

*Calling Mr. Clean.* Reprinted by permission of Karen C. Driscoll. ©2000 Karen Driscoll.

*The Unwrapped Gift.* Reprinted by permission of Sallie Rodman. ©2001 Sallie Rodman.

*To Read When You're Alone.* Reprinted by permission of Mike Staver. ©1997 Mike Staver.

*A Mother's Mid-Summer Prayer.* Reprinted by permission of Debbie Farmer. ©1998 Debbie Farmer.

*Gotta Watch the Fish Eat.* Reprinted by permission of Cheryl Kirking Kilker. ©1998 Cheryl Kirking Kilker.

*A Mother Is Born.* Reprinted by permission of Regina Phillips. ©2000 Regina Phillips.

*The Family Dinner.* Reprinted by permission of Shari Cohen. ©1997 Shari Cohen.